Keep the Lights
Burning, Abbie

Keep the Lights Burning, Abbie

by Peter and Connie Roop
pictures by
Peter E. Hanson

Carolrhoda Books · Minneapolis, Minnesota

For D.R. and Dede, who made many Maine memories possible

The artist would like to thank the Shore Village
Museum of Rockland, Maine, and especially Robert N.
Davis, curator, for providing him with information
and historical material about Matinicus Rock and the
Burgess family.

Copyright © 1985 by Carolrhoda Books, Inc.

This book is available in two editions:
Library binding by Carolrhoda Books, Inc.,
    a division of Lerner Publishing Group
Soft cover by First Avenue Editions,
    an imprint of Lerner Publishing Group
241 First Avenue North,
Minneapolis, MN 55401 U.S.A.

Website address: www.lernerbooks.com

Library of Congress Cataloging-in-Publication Data

Roop, Peter.
    Keep the lights burning, Abbie.
    (A Carolrhoda on my own book)
    Summary: In the winter of 1856, a storm delays the
lighthouse keeper's return to an island off the coast of
Maine, and his daughter Abbie must keep the lights burning
by herself.
    1. Burgess, Abbie—Juvenile literature. 2. Lighthouse
keepers—Maine—Biography—Juvenile literature.
3. Matinicus Rock Lighthouse (Matinicus Rock, Me.)—
Juvenile literature. [1. Burgess, Abbie. 2. Lighthouse
keepers] I. Roop, Connie. II. Hanson, Peter E., ill.
III. Title. IV. Series.
VK1140.B87R66 1985   387.1'55   [B] [92]   84-27446
    ISBN 0-87614-275-7 (lib. bdg. : alk. paper)
    ISBN 0-87614-454-7 (pbk. : alk. paper)

Manufactured in the United States of America
    ` 33 34 35 36 – JR – 07 06 05 04 `

A Note from the Authors

For centuries, lighthouses have warned sailors of coastal dangers. Today's lighthouse keepers have electricity, radar, and radio to aid them in their important jobs. But long ago, simple lamps and dedicated lighthouse keepers were all that kept many ships from being wrecked on hazardous rocks and ledges.

Abbie Burgess and her family moved to Matinicus Rock, off the coast of Maine, in 1853 when her father became lighthouse keeper there. On January 19, 1856, Captain Burgess went after desperately needed supplies for his family and oil for the lamps. He left Abbie in charge of the lights while he was gone. Soon after he sailed, a tremendous storm came up that lasted four weeks. During all that time, Abbie and her sisters took care of their sick mother, and Abbie kept the lights burning.

Abbie Burgess continued to take care of lighthouses for the rest of her life. Today, her grave is marked by a small lighthouse, a miniature copy of the lighthouse on Matinicus Rock.

Abbie's story is famous in the history of brave lighthouse keepers. *Keep the Lights Burning, Abbie* is based on her own accounts of the storm and on information from other historical sources.

Abbie looked out the lighthouse window.
Waves washed up on the rocks below.
Out at sea, a ship sailed safely by.

"Will you sail to town today, Papa?"
Abbie asked.

"Yes," Captain Burgess answered.

"Mama needs medicine.

The lights need oil.

We need food.

The weather is good now.

So it's safe to go out in *Puffin*."

"But what if you don't get back today?"
asked Abbie.

"Who will take care of the lights?"
Papa smiled.

"You will, Abbie."

"Oh, no, Papa!" said Abbie.

"I have never done it alone."

"You have trimmed the wicks before,"
said Papa.
"You have cleaned the lamps
and put in the oil.
Mama is too sick to do it.
Your sisters are too little.
You must keep the lights burning, Abbie.
Many ships count on our lighthouses."
Abbie followed Papa down the steps.
Another day, she would have raced.
This morning, her legs felt
too heavy to run.

She and Papa walked
down to the shore.
Their little boat, *Puffin*,
pulled on its rope.
Captain Burgess jumped into the boat.
He raised the sail.
Puffin moved away from the shore.

"Keep the lights burning, Abbie!"
her father called.
"I will, Papa," Abbie cried.
But the wind carried off her words.
Abbie watched *Puffin* slide out to sea.
Far away, she could see
Matinicus Island.

She knew Papa was a fine sailor.
He could sail in rain.
He could sail in fog.
But if the wind blew up again,
he could not sail back
to Matinicus Rock today.
The waves would be too high
for the little boat.
Then she would have to
care for the lights.
Abbie looked up.
The two lighthouse towers
seemed as high as the sky.

Her family's stone house
sat between the towers.
Not far away stood Abbie's henhouse.

Abbie went to feed her chickens.

She threw some corn on the ground.

The hungry hens hurried to it.

Abbie sat on a rock and watched them.

"Now listen, Hope, Patience, and Charity,"
she said.

"Don't eat it all too fast.

There is not much corn left.

But Papa will bring you more."

Abbie sighed.

"I hope he gets home today.

I am a little afraid

to care for the lights alone."

Patience pecked Abbie's shoe.

Hope turned her head.

Charity ruffled her feathers.

Abbie laughed.

"You three always make me feel better."

Abbie walked to the house.

Esther opened the door.

"When is Papa coming back?" she asked.

"This afternoon," said Abbie.

"What if another storm starts?"
asked Mahala.

"Don't worry," Abbie told her.

"Papa will come back as soon as he can.
You two run and get the eggs.
How is Mama?"
Abbie asked her sister Lydia.

"Still too sick to get up,"
Lydia answered.

"It's a good thing Papa went today.
Mama needs medicine.
And we are running out of food."

"Then we must be careful," said Abbie.

"If there is another storm,
Papa will not get back today.
We must make the food last."

That afternoon, Abbie helped Mahala
write her letters.
Esther helped Lydia cook supper.
Everyone helped take care of Mama.

Outside, the sky turned gray.
The wind put whitecaps on the waves.
Another winter storm was coming.
When the sun went down,
Abbie put on her coat.
She had to light the lamps.

Abbie ran up the lighthouse steps.

She stopped at the top to look out.

The waves were like big hills.

The wind blew rain at the windows.

She could not even see Matinicus Island.

She knew Papa could not sail back.

Abbie was afraid.

She wished her brother, Benjy,

were home.

But he was away fishing.

What if she could not light the lamps?

She picked up a box of matches.
Her hands were shaking.
She struck a match, but it went out.
She struck another. This one burned.
Abbie held the match
near the wick of the first lamp.
The wick glowed.
The light made Abbie feel better.
One by one, she lit all the lamps.
Then she went to the other
lighthouse tower.
She lit those lamps as well.
Out at sea, a ship saw the lights.
It steered away
from the dangerous rocks.

That night, the wind blew hard.

Abbie could not sleep.

She kept thinking about the lights.

What if they went out?

A ship might crash.

Abbie got out of bed.

She put on her coat.

She climbed the lighthouse steps.

It was a good thing she had come.

There was ice on the windows.

The lights could not be seen.

All night long,

Abbie climbed up and down.

She scraped ice off the windows.

She checked each light.

Not one went out.

In the morning, the wind still blew.

Waves rolled across Matinicus Rock.

Abbie blew out each light.

She trimmed each wick.

She cleaned each lamp.

She put in more oil.

Then she went to breakfast.

Then, at last, she went to bed.

For over a week,
the wind and rain roared.
For a while, the family had to move
into one of the strong towers.
One morning, water ran under the door.
"My chickens!" Abbie cried.
"They will be washed away."

"Don't go outside," said Lydia.

"You will be washed away, too."

Abbie picked up a basket.

"I go outside every night," she said.

"I haven't been washed away yet."

She opened the door.

Water splashed into the room.

Abbie ran out into the rain.

She waded to the henhouse.

She put Patience under one arm.

She pushed Hope and Charity
into the basket.

Just then she heard
another big wave coming.

It sounded like a train!

Abbie raced to the tower.

"Open the door!" she yelled.

Lydia opened the door.

Abbie ran inside.

"Oh, look!" Mahala cried.

"Look there!

The sea is coming!"

The wave crashed over Matinicus Rock.
It washed away the henhouse.
The girls pushed the door shut.
Then the wave hit it.
Abbie felt the lighthouse shake.
She was shaking, too.
They had shut the door just in time.

Day after day, it snowed or rained.
Abbie wished it would stop.
She was tired of the wind.
She was tired of the waves.
She was tired of climbing
the lighthouse steps.

And she was tired of eggs.
The only thing left to eat was eggs,
and Abbie was sick of them.

Then one morning,
the waves seemed smaller.
The sky was not so black.
The wind did not blow so hard.
Late that afternoon,
the girls heard a voice outside.

It was Papa.

They ran to help him carry in the boxes.

There was medicine for Mama.

There was oil for the lamps.

There was mail, and there was food.

And there was corn for Abbie's chickens.

"I was afraid for you," said Papa.

"Every night I watched for the lights.

Every night I saw them.

Then I knew you were all right."

Abbie smiled.

"I kept the lights burning, Papa."